TWENTY

21 DAYS WITH JESUS

ONE

JERRY LAWSON

ENDORSEMENTS

"Jerry Lawson is a pastor, leader and communicator, but most of all he is a disciple of Jesus. These twenty-one personal devotions expose his heart. I have read them, every one! They are the observations, applications and prayers of a true follower of Christ.

They are fresh, written from a hungry heart after Christ. They are challenging, with probing questions that make us examine ourselves. They are Word-Centered, cutting through our misplaced values to reveal the only Truth and Life that really matters...Jesus Christ!

Wow! It really is '21 Days with Jesus.'"

Dr. Raymond Culpepper
Author/Pastor/Administrative Bishop
Church of God, Alabama

"In '21 Days With Jesus,' Pastor Jerry Lawson takes you on a journey that shines a spotlight on the heart of God for us. Every page drips with Jerry's incredible ability to communicate deep truths in such a clear way. Take the journey! You will never be the same!"

Acton Bowen
Communicator/Author

"All of us need an occasional boost in our daily time alone with God. Help has arrived! I am privileged to know Jerry Lawson— author of this '21 Days with Jesus' devotional book — and I can vouch for his authentic relationship with Christ that is contagious to his family and friends. In reading this book, you will be encouraged, challenged, and captured by the timeless truths and wonderful insights contained within. Jerry helps us apply the scriptures to our lives in practical ways. Dive deeply into this great resource and prepare to grow stronger in your relationship with Jesus."

Ed Funderburk
Executive Pastor, CONNECT
A ministry for pastors and churches
Gateway Church

"Jerry Lawson is not only a personal friend, but a colleague in the ministry. This is a book that will encourage you to spend more time with the Lord—this is a road worth traveling and sorely needed in today's church."

Marcus D. Lamb
Founder – President
Daystar Television Network

To Leslie,
the best thing to ever happen
to me!

CONTENTS

FOREWORD

The title, "21 Days With Jesus," sounds like heaven on earth! We all look forward to the time when we spend all our days with Jesus, but until then, Jerry Lawson has given us some daily nourishment. In this little book, Lawson shares knowledge and spiritual insights he gleaned from those precious moments in intimacy with Christ. He encourages the reader not to be blinded by our own rules and spirits of religion, but to understand - it is always simply about Jesus and Jesus is always about people.

Jerry Lawson is well qualified to write about spending time with Jesus. He began preaching at a young age, and became the senior pastor of his first church at the age of 19. Currently, he serves as the founding pastor of Daystar Church in Cullman, Alabama which is a megachurch.
Jerry Lawson is not only a personal friend, but a colleague in the ministry. This is a book that will encourage you to spend more time with the Lord—this is a road worth traveling and sorely needed in today's church.

Marcus D. Lamb
Founder – President
Daystar Television Network

The truth is, for most of my Christian walk, I never journaled. As a new believer, no one ever told me I should. In the years that followed, as much as I tried to be faithful in journaling, I never consistently stuck with it. When I became a pastor, well-meaning church people would often give me one of those "pastor journals" for Christmas or pastor's appreciation day. They had places to record all the "preacher activities" like weddings, funerals and special occasions. I never filled in one line. I would just try to have a daily quiet time with God and think of something to write if I had time. Eventually, that new "pastor journal" would go the way of all those before it and be set aside. I felt guilty and ashamed that I did not journal properly, like most of my church members probably thought I was doing.

As I went deeper into ministry and into my walk with Christ, I did become more consistent in journaling, but I never really knew what I was doing. And frankly, I wasn't even sure why I was doing it. I would write a little each day. It may be a testimony or a prayer request or an occasional insight from my prayer and devotional time, but still, my journaling lacked purpose and meaning.

In 2011, I joined a coaching network for pastors offered by Perry Noble. Perry is the pastor of an exciting church in South Carolina called NewSpring Church. His controversial reputation preceded him, but shortly after I met him and got to know him a little better, I learned of another side. I found out that Perry's life was truly directed by his devotional time. Everyone around him said so. I remember walking past his opened Bible one day and it looked like he had written more personal observations in the margins than were in the actual text. I could see that he was a man of God's Word, and it inspired me to go deeper.

While in that mentoring relationship with Perry, I learned of his personal struggles with depression. Perry gave me a book called, *Leading on Empty* by Wayne Cordiero. As soon as I saw the cover, I knew that this book was for me. I was truly leading on empty. About a year later, I took my first ministry sabbatical and finally got around to reading *Leading on Empty*. The book changed my life. I have since given away nearly 100 copies to other pastors and leaders. Wayne's story taught me so much. What I learned most was that a daily quiet time with God, a time that I listen to Him and record what He says to me, is really the fuel to keep my life going. In the years since this realization, I have faced many struggles and fears. There have been times I wanted to give up and even searched for some way out. But it has been my private time with God that has brought me through.

This book is simply my attempt at sharing some of the most precious and powerful moments of my life with you. These twenty-one devotionals are straight from my prayer journals. I have chosen some of my favorite moments with Jesus. These are the moments that have fueled my journey and I pray that they will inspire you to love Him more and stay in His presence as long as you can.

INTRODUCTION

Jesus Christ is the most controversial figure in all of human history. He came from a remote, poverty-stricken village and never traveled far from there. He spent his time with the lowest class of people and chose to train twelve of the least likely of candidates to carry on His work after Him. After spending just over three years with these men, Jesus was taken away from them and publically humiliated and murdered. Yet this man changed the face of human history forever. There simply is no one like Jesus.

Christ's words were recorded, in part, by four simple men. These men were untrained, uneducated and certainly not professional writers. And yet, those words have produced some of the most amazing actions from their readers. Kings and countries have gone to war over the words of Christ. Men and women have sacrificed their lives because of these words. Futures have been altered, love has been ignited, and sin has been forgiven all because of the words of Christ in the New Testament.

Over the next twenty-one days, I ask you to take a journey with me through some of the most amazing words Jesus spoke or were spoken of Him. You will find, as I have, that Jesus is not just one of many gods. He is not one of many paths to heaven. He is everything He claimed to be when He said, "I am the way and the truth and the life. No one comes to the Father except through me" (John 14:6, NIV).

This book is a quick read and you could probably read it all in one setting. But don't do that. The words I have written in this book came to me (I believe from heaven) because I set aside daily time to spend with Jesus. And He honored that sacrifice by joining me daily and opening His word up to me. I believe that I have captured His heart in the pages that follow. And I am praying that, as you set aside time for God and His word, you will sense His presence with you also.

TORN IN HALF

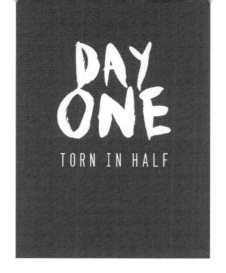

DAY ONE

TORN IN HALF

SCRIPTURE

Luke 23:44-46 MSG
By now it was noon. The whole earth became dark, the darkness lasting three hours—a total blackout. The Temple curtain split right down the middle. Jesus called loudly, "Father, I place my life in your hands!" Then he breathed his last.

OBSERVATION

These words are Luke's telling of the last seconds of Jesus' life on the cross. This was a historic event, indeed. It defined the future of all mankind. The text tells us that the temple curtain was split. This was both a physical miracle and a symbol of a larger spiritual truth. This temple curtain was a large woven piece of fabric that separated the Holy of Holies from the rest of the temple where men dwelt. It was sixty feet high and four inches thick.

Historian Josephus said that horses tied to each side could not pull the veil apart. The curtain was so imposing to show just how separate God was from sinful man. But Jesus coming to earth was the solution to our separation. More significant than the physical tearing of cloth was the fact that through Jesus' substitutionary death on the cross, we can now come before this holy God knowing that Jesus has dealt with our sin problem.

What happened in the spirit world bled into the natural world, as the physical curtain that separated man from the presence of God was literally torn in half!

JESUS CALLED LOUDLY,
"FATHER, I PLACE MY LIFE IN
YOUR HANDS!"

APPLICATION

I have complete access to go before a 100% holy God, even in my unholiness. It is, in fact, my faith that makes me righteous in His eyes. I will cry out to Him early and often, knowing that He hears me <u>every time</u>, no matter what my physical reasoning and emotion tell me. I will never doubt that I belong in God's presence because to do so would make useless Christ's sacrifice on the cross.

PRAYER

God, make me hungry for Your presence. Help me to come before Your throne with prayer and petition. Thank You for the sacrifice which made this possible. And forgive me for the times I have not taken advantage of the privilege you died to give me.

RULES OR
RELATIONSHIP?

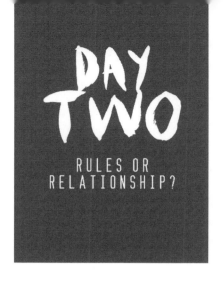

DAY TWO

RULES OR RELATIONSHIP?

SCRIPTURE

John 5:1-16 NKJV

After this there was a feast of the Jews, and Jesus went up to Jerusalem. 2 Now there is in Jerusalem by the Sheep Gate a pool, which is called in Hebrew, Bethesda, having five porches. 3 In these lay a great multitude of sick people, blind, lame, paralyzed, waiting for the moving of the water. 4 For an angel went down at a certain time into the pool and stirred up the water; then whoever stepped in first, after the stirring of the water, was made well of whatever disease he had. 5 Now a certain man was there who had an infirmity thirty-eight years. 6 When Jesus saw him lying there, and knew that he already had been in that condition a long time, He said to him, "Do you want to be made well?" 7 The sick man answered Him, "Sir, I have no man to put me into the pool when the water is stirred up; but while I am coming, another steps down before me." 8 Jesus said to him, "Rise, take up your bed and walk." 9 And immediately the man was made well, took up his bed, and walked. And that day was the Sabbath. 10 The Jews therefore said to him who was cured, "It is the Sabbath; it is not lawful for you to carry your bed." 11 He answered them, "He who made me well said to me, 'Take up your bed and walk.'" 12 Then they asked him, "Who is the Man who said to you, 'Take up your bed and walk'?" 13 But the one who was healed did not know who it was, for Jesus had withdrawn, a multitude being in that place. 14 Afterward Jesus found him in the temple, and said to him, "See, you have been made well. Sin no more, lest a worse thing come upon you." 15 The man departed and told the Jews that it was Jesus who had made him well. 16 For this reason the Jews persecuted Jesus, and sought to kill Him, because He had done these things on the Sabbath.

OBSERVATION

In this story, Jesus has just encountered a man who had been lame for thirty-eight years. Jesus healed him and told him to take up his mat and walk home. But the act of carrying the mat was seen as a violation of the Sabbath, as was Jesus' act of healing the man. The religious leaders were so in love with the rules that they actually wanted to kill Jesus for this. The religious leaders of Jesus' day seem to have no concern for the person in this story. What about the fact that a man disabled for thirty-eight years is now whole? This doesn't even seem to matter to them. They cannot see the purpose for the gospel because they are so blinded by their own rules.

JESUS SAID TO HIM,
"RISE, TAKE UP YOUR BED AND WALK."
AND IMMEDIATELY THE MAN WAS MADE WELL
TOOK UP HIS BED, AND WALKED.

APPLICATION

The spirit of religion is so powerful that it blinds us to our own ignorance. I would like to say that this is a problem that only existed in Jesus' day and is now gone, but the fact is, religion continues to stand as a modern substitute for relationship even today. And if Jesus didn't kill the spirit of religion, I know I cannot either. I will have to fight it for my entire life. It will always be about rules and ritual, while Jesus is always about the people.

TOUGH QUESTIONS THE TEXT DEMANDS

1. How can I be sure that I never substitute ritual and religion for a true vibrant, passionate relationship with Jesus?

2. Am I seeking God's word for what it says and for His presence in my life regularly, so I will not drift toward the powerful influence of religion in our world today?

PRAYER

I take authority over the spirit of religion today. It has no place in my life, my family, my church, and my ministry. I repent of any times that I, my team, our leaders or our church has, in any way, allowed the spirit of religion to influence us. I invite the Spirit of God to fill us completely. Come to the places where religion once occupied and make it Your home, Jesus. May our hearts always burn for You and Your presence.

DAY THREE

**JESUS, THE WORLD'S
GREATEST
CHANGE-AGENT**

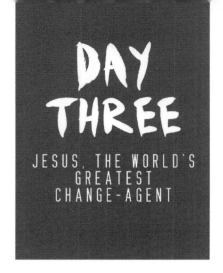

DAY THREE

JESUS, THE WORLD'S GREATEST CHANGE-AGENT

SCRIPTURE

Acts 4:8-12 NKJV

Then Peter, filled with the Holy Spirit, said to them, "Rulers of the people, and elders of Israel, if we this day are judged for a good deed done to a helpless man, by what means he has been made well, let it be made known to you all, and to all the people in Israel, that by the name of Jesus Christ of Nazareth, whom you crucified, whom God raised from the dead, by Him this man stands before you whole. This is the 'stone which was rejected by you builders, which has become the chief cornerstone.' Nor is there salvation in any other, for there is no other name under heaven given among men by which we must be saved."

OBSERVATION

These words of Peter are just a sample of the dramatic change that happened in the disciples following the resurrection. Remember that the very people Peter is now telling so boldly that Jesus is the only source for salvation, are the ones he ran from before the resurrection. Here, after Christ has risen, Peter is so BOLD and FEARLESS. Clearly, Jesus was no ordinary man. How could a man bring about such a change in others? This had to be the only Son of God.

"THIS IS THE STONE WHICH WAS REJECTED BY YOU BUILDERS, WHICH HAS BECOME THE CHIEF CORNERSTONE."

APPLICATION

In my travels, I have encountered many different religious systems and world views. However, they have only further convinced me that they lack the one missing piece of the puzzle - Jesus Christ! The truth is, many of the world's religions share deep similarities. And even Christianity shares some similarities with other faiths. But no other belief system has a JESUS! The truth is, there is no one like Jesus. He trumps everything else.

Jesus changes all arguments, and Jesus changes people like no one else in the world. When I know there is some area of my life that needs positive change, my task is to just get as close to Him as possible. In the case of Peter,

He makes the cowardly, courageous. In the case of Matthew, He makes a sinner a saint. Look at the case of Paul; he turned a church persecutor into a church pioneer. On and on the stories go from the earliest disciples to today's Christ followers. Jesus is the source of all redemptive change in our lives.

TOUGH QUESTIONS
THE TEXT DEMANDS

1. Given Jesus' propensity to bring about dynamic redemptive change, what changes are happening in my life now as a result of Christ's presence?

2. Can I think of anything that needs to be changed in me, but I have been resistant of Jesus' efforts to bring about that change? What is it? Why?

3. What can I do to open myself up to more of Christ's plan of redemption in my life?

PRAYER

Thank you, Jesus, for being who You are. As I serve You more and more, You become even more real to me. I am utterly convinced that You are real and that there simply is no one like You in all the heavens or the earth. Thank You for loving me, healing me, cleansing me and just being so patient with me. And please help me to draw nearer to Your true heart. With all that is in me, I love You, Lord.

DAY FOUR

PASSION FOR
CHRIST

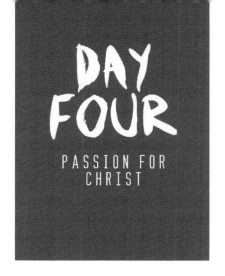

DAY FOUR

PASSION FOR CHRIST

SCRIPTURE

John 21:1-8 NKJV

After these things Jesus showed Himself again to the disciples at the Sea of Tiberias, and in this way He showed Himself: 2 Simon Peter, Thomas called the Twin, Nathanael of Cana in Galilee, the sons of Zebedee, and two others of His disciples were together. 3 Simon Peter said to them, "I am going fishing." They said to him, "We are going with you also." They went out and immediately got into the boat, and that night they caught nothing. 4 But when the morning had now come, Jesus stood on the shore; yet the disciples did not know that it was Jesus. 5 Then Jesus said to them, "Children, have you any food?" They answered Him, "No."

6 And He said to them, "Cast the net on the right side of the boat, and you will find some." So they cast, and now they were not able to draw it in because of the multitude of fish. 7 Therefore that disciple whom Jesus loved said to Peter, "It is the Lord!" Now when Simon Peter heard that

it was the Lord, he put on his outer garment (for he had removed it), and plunged into the sea. 8 But the other disciples came in the little boat (for they were not far from land, but about two hundred cubits), dragging the net with fish.

OBSERVATION

On a recent trip to Israel, I was able to literally see and touch the water these men were in. I visualized that small boat the disciples were in and what it must have looked like when Peter left its comfort for the opportunity to once again see Jesus. Just from reading the text, one can see the passion for Christ from Peter and John. The very instant that Peter realizes that this is Jesus, he leaves his boat, his friends, and his catch and swims the length of a football field to get to Jesus first. And years later, when John recounts the events of that day, he can only refer to himself as "the disciple whom Jesus loved." Oh, can't you just feel the love John had for this man whom he was certain could love no one as much as he did him? Jesus is certainly the most moving figure in human history. These men, who had almost lost Him, are willing to do anything to have Him back in their lives.

APPLICATION

I want to match Peter's passion for Christ in my life. I want to always be the first one to jump out of the boat when we realize that Jesus isn't in it. I want to be the one who expels all of my energy racing to His feet. I want to set the pace that all others follow. And like the Apostle Paul, 2,000 years ago, I want to so passionately follow Christ that it is one day said that he "turned the city upside down for Jesus"

(Acts 17). During my time in Israel, my heart was crushed time after time as I heard the blinded Jews talk all around Jesus and yet not notice Him in the very scriptures they so passionately embrace. I want to so feverishly chase after Jesus that others will want to know what is so special about this man.

TOUGH QUESTIONS THE TEXT DEMANDS

1. Is there any part of my life where I am sailing in a boat while Jesus is on the shore?

2. How can I quickly get out of that boat and onto the shore with Jesus?

3. Do I, like John, take the time to linger in Jesus' presence? What is stopping me? Why am I in such a hurry to leave His side?

PRAYER

Lord, I am so inspired by the passion of Peter and John, and I want to be just like them. Peter always followed His first impulse to chase after You, and John always lingered in your presence as long as he could. Lord, let me be the FIRST ONE out of the boat every time and the LAST ONE to leave Your breast. I want to be both Peter and John. I love You so much, Jesus. You are so real to me. Thank You for being so forgiving, so gracious and so patient with me. Thank You for being my Friend and allowing me to call You by name.

DAY FIVE

REWARD OF THE

FAITHFUL

REWARD OF THE
FAITHFUL

SCRIPTURE

Luke 19:11-26 NLT

11 The crowd was listening to everything Jesus said. And because he was nearing Jerusalem, he told them a story to correct the impression that the Kingdom of God would begin right away. 12 He said, "A nobleman was called away to a distant empire to be crowned king and then return. 13 Before he left, he called together ten of his servants and divided among them ten pounds of silver, saying, 'Invest this for me while I am gone.' 14 But his people hated him and sent a delegation after him to say, 'We do not want him to be our king.'

15 "After he was crowned king, he returned and called in the servants to whom he had given the money. He wanted to find out what their profits were. 16 The first servant reported, 'Master, I invested your money and made ten times the original amount!' 17 "'Well done!' the king exclaimed. 'You are a good servant. You have been faithful with the little I entrusted to you, so you will be governor

of ten cities as your reward.' 18 "The next servant reported, 'Master, I invested your money and made five times the original amount.' 19 "'Well done!' the king said. 'You will be governor over five cities.' 20 "But the third servant brought back only the original amount of money and said, 'Master, I hid your money and kept it safe. 21 I was afraid because you are a hard man to deal with, taking what isn't yours and harvesting crops you didn't plant.' 22 "'You wicked servant!' the king roared. 'Your own words condemn you. If you knew that I'm a hard man who takes what isn't mine and harvests crops I didn't plant, 23 why didn't you deposit my money in the bank? At least I could have gotten some interest on it.' 24 "Then, turning to the others standing nearby, the king ordered, 'Take the money from this servant, and give it to the one who has ten pounds.' 25 "'But, master,' they said, 'he already has ten pounds!' 26 "'Yes,' the king replied, 'and to those who use well what they are given, even more will be given. But from those who do nothing, even what little they have will be taken away.'"

OBSERVATION

So much of what we believe about Jesus is less a product of His words and more a product of what we wish Him to be. In fact, I have often said that instead of us rejoicing in the fact that we are made in His image, we seem to continue to try to remake God into our image. This is one of those "Jesus stories" that reveals that in some ways He is not so politically correct as we would like Him to be. In this parable, Jesus tells of people who "have" as well as people who "have not," and He lands on a side that might surprise many of His followers today. This teaching reveals Jesus' philosophy on investing in people. At least in this passage, He does not seem to be moved by the fact that someone has less than others. However, he is moved to anger when those He has given to, do little or nothing with His investment. Rather than taking from the rich and giving it to the poor, Jesus takes from those who have less and actually gives it to those who have more.

Now, no one would argue that Jesus does not, in many other places in Scripture, call on us to give to the poor. However, this lesson from Jesus is important lest we forget that He places a high priority on working hard, particularly for His Kingdom.

APPLICATION

This story speaks to me in at least two ways. First, I want to be sure that I am faithful with what God invests in me. The Bible teaches us that God requires much out of those to whom He has given much (Luke 12:48). And here, in this parable, we learn that when we are faithful with what He gives us, we get more. Simply put, I want to be in position to receive even more blessings from heaven.

Secondly, I want to lead like Jesus. Never forget that Jesus is the greatest leader the world has ever known. He literally took twelve nobodies from nowhere, spent three years with them in remote and obscure places and literally changed the world through them. He is the Leader that all leaders should emulate. If I do, in fact, lead like Jesus, I will make sure that those I'm depending on are producers. And when they are productive, it is my task to give them more resources and more responsibility. However, when they are not productive, it will be my responsibility to take away resources and responsibilities to transfer them to the productive.

PRAYER

Lord, I realize that you have graciously chosen to invest much into me. I pray that I am a good investment for Your kingdom. Help me to be worthy of that trust. And help me to position myself in a place where I can receive an even greater investment.

A BANK THAT CAN'T
GO BANKRUPT

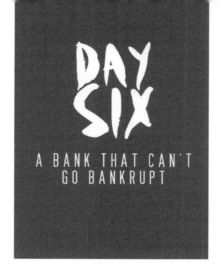

DAY SIX

A BANK THAT CAN'T GO BANKRUPT

SCRIPTURE

Luke 12:29-34 MSG

29-32 What I'm trying to do here is get you to relax, not be so preoccupied with getting so you can respond to God's giving. People who don't know God and the way he works fuss over these things, but you know both God and how he works. Steep yourself in God-reality, God-initiative, God-provisions. You'll find all your everyday human concerns will be met. Don't be afraid of missing out. You're my dearest friends! The Father wants to give you the very kingdom itself.

33-34 "Be generous. Give to the poor. Get yourselves a bank that can't go bankrupt, a bank in heaven far from bankrobbers, safe from embezzlers, a bank you can bank on. It's obvious, isn't it? The place where your treasure is, is the place you will most want to be, and end up being."

OBSERVATION

Jesus continues here to drive home the point of a longer discourse that loving money is pointless. Earlier He says, "Life is not defined by what you have, even when you have a lot." It appears that not much has changed in 2,000 years. The very issues that Jesus spent much of His time teaching about still cause so many to stumble today. For today, people still gauge their lives based on money and possessions.

"BE GENEROUS. GIVE TO THE POOR. GET YOURSELVES A BANK THAT CAN'T GO BANKRUPT, A BANK IN HEAVEN FAR FROM BANKROBBERS, SAFE FROM EMBEZZLERS, A BANK YOU CAN BANK ON.

APPLICATION

The task of Western believers today is to avoid the trap Jesus warned us of in this teaching. Our lives are not measured by the amount of money or possessions we can accumulate. However, Jesus thought it so difficult a battle that He actually taught more on money, possessions and greed than any other subject. He introduced the world to a fact that many have come to prove true: "Where your treasure is, there your heart will be also."

TOUGH QUESTIONS THE TEXT DEMANDS

1. In the above passage Jesus directly commands me to be generous. How am I doing at that?

2. Since the excuse for not being generous is usually that we lack the funds to do so, where can I specifically eliminate unnecessary spending, so I can have more capacity to be generous?

3. Since a lack of generosity is a lack of faith, what can I do to stretch my own faith?

PRAYER

Lord, thank You for your amazing generosity toward us all. When you saw the world in trouble, you loved us so much that you "gave." And what you gave to us was the best that heaven had to offer. Help us to follow your example and cultivate a culture of generosity, first within our hearts and families and later within Your Church.

DAY SEVEN

SUPREME HYPOCRISY

DAY SEVEN

SUPREME HYPOCRISY

SCRIPTURE

Luke 20:45-47 MSG
With everybody listening, Jesus spoke to his disciples. "Watch out for the religion scholars. They love to walk around in academic gowns, preen in the radiance of public flattery, bask in prominent positions, sit at the head table at every church function. And all the time they are exploiting the weak and helpless. The longer their prayers, the worse they get. But they'll pay for it in the end."

OBSERVATION

Stories like this make me love Jesus all the more. While all of the sanctimonious parading around was going on, Jesus chose not to participate. In fact, He was not even guilty of giving tacit approval. Instead, He boldly spoke up "with everybody listening" and called the hypocrites out for the pretenders that they were. Although the times have changed, we still have pious "honor-seekers" in our church culture today. They have self-righteous talk and deceive so many. It's a picture of injustice, the very sin Jesus came to destroy.

> "THE GREATEST AMONG YOU WILL
> BE YOUR SERVANT"
> MATTHEW 23:11

APPLICATION

As a Christian leader in a world full of skeptics, I must be keenly aware of my responsibility. Jesus made it clear to His followers that we are not called to the spiritually healthy, but to the sick. So we do have to care what they think of us. And there must not be a hint of self-righteousness or pious arrogance. Rather than take our place at the head table, we must defer to someone else. Remember, Jesus did not come to be served, but to serve. And if I am to be His follower I must seek to serve always. It was Jesus who said, "The greatest among you will be your servant" (Mt 23:11).

My goal for my church and for my life is to be the exact opposite of this. God resists the proud, but He gives grace to the humble. There are many ways to be too proud, but no way to be too humble. God always lifts up those who humble themselves before Him.

TOUGH QUESTIONS
THE TEXT DEMANDS

1. It is so easy to spot hypocrisy in others, but almost impossible to spot it in myself. What am I doing to make sure that none of my ways are ever hypocritical?

2. Since hypocrites become hypocrites by spending all of their time with other hypocrites, how many outright lost people do I regularly talk to? What am I doing to expend my influence among the un saved?

PRAYER

Lord, help me grow in humility before you, looking out for the poor, the widow, the orphan and the sick. I truly want to finish the work that You began here on earth. So help me to continue to show your love to the spiritually sick in my circle of influence.

DAY EIGHT

REDEMPTIVE HEALING

DAY EIGHT

REDEMPTIVE HEALING

SCRIPTURE

Luke 5:22 – 26 MSG

Jesus knew exactly what they were thinking and said, "Why all this gossipy whispering? Which is simpler: to say 'I forgive your sins,' or to say 'Get up and start walking'? Well, just so it's clear that I'm the Son of Man and authorized to do either, or both. . . ." He now spoke directly to the paraplegic: "Get up. Take your bedroll and go home." Without a moment's hesitation, he did it—got up, took his blanket, and left for home, giving glory to God all the way. The people rubbed their eyes, incredulous—and then also gave glory to God. Awestruck, they said, "We've never seen anything like that!"

OBSERVATION

"We've never seen anything like that!" This may have been the understatement of all understatements. In chapter five of Luke, Jesus performed the following miracles: (1) filled Peter's nets with fish, (2) healed a terminal "incurable" leper, (3) healed a paraplegic.

I don't know about you, but I certainly have never seen anything like that before. But performing miracles was really only half of what amazed the crowd. What excited and infuriated many was the fact that Jesus was so bold as to forgive sins, something only God can do. But for Christ to heal and not forgive would go against His divine purpose. All of the healing Jesus did, He did for redemptive purposes.

When He preaches to the crowd on the beach, He forgives the sins of the paralyzed man before healing Him. And in that same setting He says, "I'm here inviting outsiders, not insiders – an invitation to a changed life, changed inside and out." And we see that the healings were not just about healing, at all. In fact, they were about drawing attention to Who He was – the Christ. And His ultimate purpose was not just to heal physical ailments, but to heal mankind of our sin infection.

APPLICATION

Today the Church world is all over the map on the subject of divine healing. Some go so far as to say that God no longer performs physical healings. However, that is a position that is hard to support with Scripture. While many other believers still know that God can and does heal, most are unsure why He does it. But the answer is quite simple. Since Jesus Christ is the same, yesterday, today and forever, He still heals today; and He still does it for the same reason that He did before. Jesus Christ heals people, not for physical purposes, but for redemptive purposes. Ultimately, Christ was sent to earth to redeem the souls of men and that is why He does everything that He does. He teaches, heals and inspires for redemptive purposes.

> THE PEOPLE RUBBED THEIR EYES, INCREDULOUS — AND THEN ALSO GAVE GLORY TO GOD. AWESTRUCK, THEY SAID, "WE'VE NEVER SEEN ANYTHING LIKE THAT!"

While some believers get so enamored with the power of Christ's healing that they forget it is all for nothing if the lost are not getting saved. Others, sadly, are so evangelistic that they forget that our God is still "the Great Physician" that Saint Luke observed. God still wants to "wow" people by healing the sick and saving the most unlikely of characters. He does not heal the sick so a faith healer can become famous and sell out giant arenas all over the world. Neither does He forgive sinners so pastors can have bigger and bigger churches to build their egos. Jesus made it clear that the purpose of all that He does is to "bring in the outsiders." God is a redemptive God; therefore, everything He does has redemptive purposes, redeeming His lost children.

PRAYER

Lord, I ask for more miracles, more healing, and more salvation of the utterly lost and outcast. Make Your Church today a more redemptive church and make us a more redemptive people. Help us to stretch our faith and believe for more miracles and more life-change by Your power. May we always follow Your model of weaving the miraculous acts of God in with the redemptive purposes of God.

DAY NINE

ROOM FOR THE
BLIND AND
CRIPPLED

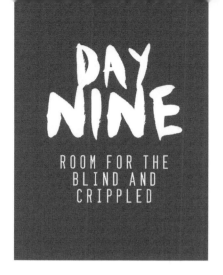

DAY NINE

ROOM FOR THE BLIND AND CRIPPLED

SCRIPTURE

Matthew 21:12 – 14 MSG
Jesus went straight to the Temple and threw out everyone who had set up shop, buying and selling. He kicked over the tables of loan sharks and the stalls of dove merchants. He quoted this text:
"My house was designated a house of prayer;
You have made it a hangout for thieves."
Now there was room for the blind and crippled to get in. They came to Jesus and he healed them.

OBSERVATION

The many times we hear reference to this "Jesus story" emphasis is often placed on the selling of merchandise. However, a closer look at the story reveals that Jesus' actions are not simply motivated by the selling of goods in God's house, but rather by thievery. And mostly, He is incensed by the fact that this behavior was keeping the blind and the crippled out. This was probably because they did not have the money to pay the temple tax administered by these "thieves and loan sharks."

APPLICATION

Since Jesus is so angered by injustice that keeps the poor and needy away from His presence, it is important that we always be aware of how our decisions and actions affect the needy. God will not bless anything that does not reflect His heart. It really doesn't matter where you open up the bible and begin reading, you will not get far without hearing the heart of God caring for those in need. Simply put, I cannot be like Jesus if I do not have His heart for the poor and needy. Further, there is not a more dangerous place to be than standing between Christ and those who need Him. In fact, this account brings to memory Christ's words to the Pharisees in Matthew 23:

"WOE TO YOU, TEACHERS OF THE LAW AND PHARISEES, YOU HYPOCRITES! YOU SHUT THE DOOR OF THE KINGDOM OF HEAVEN IN PEOPLE'S FACES. YOU YOURSELVES DO NOT ENTER, NOR WILL YOU LET THOSE ENTER WHO ARE TRYING TO."
MATTHEW 23:13 NIV

PRAYER

Lord, help me to slow down and reflect on how I live my life as a believer and Christian leader. It is my responsibility to never stand in the way of those who would reach out to Christ, and further to reach out to the needy on His behalf. I pray that I will always be motivated by Your love and that I will catch your heart. Finally, Lord, send the blind and crippled my way so that I can have the privilege of being your hands and heart extended.

DAY TEN

WHO AM I
IN CHRIST?

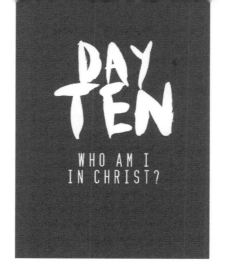

DAY TEN

WHO AM I
IN CHRIST?

SCRIPTURE

Ephesians 1:11 – 12 MSG
It's in Christ that we find out who we are and what we are living for. Long before we first heard of Christ and got our hopes up, he had his eye on us, had designs on us for glorious living, part of the overall purpose he is working out in everything and everyone.

OBSERVATION

As the Apostle Paul writes to those whom he has recently introduced to Christ for the very first time, he tells them that they are a part of a great big divine plan that involves everyone and everything. How exciting that must have been for that entire community to come to understand the depths of God's great plan together. They were learning that God had been pursuing them long before they turned to Him. And that they were a part of His great plan for all of humanity.

APPLICATION

Just like the Ephesian believers of Paul's day, I actually can never understand who I am apart from Christ. My real identity is in Christ alone. It really doesn't matter what others think of me or how they perceive me. The only way to know who I really am and to know what I'm to do with my life is to draw closer to Christ.

TOUGH QUESTIONS
THE TEXT DEMANDS

1. When I look at myself in the mirror what do I see? Can I honestly say I see myself as Christ does?

2. Do I allow competing voices to speak to me about my worth and value?

3. Do I really believe that I am *chosen by God, made in God's image, set apart for greatness*? Or do I struggle to believe such words?

PRAYER

Lord, help me to see through Your eyes, mostly to see myself through Your eyes. I further ask You to help me walk closer to You, so I can become and do all that You have planned for me.

DAY ELEVEN

WHEN FAITH LEAKS

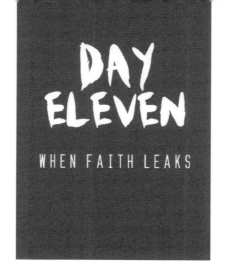

DAY ELEVEN

WHEN FAITH LEAKS

SCRIPTURE

Luke 24:12 – 16 MSG
That same day two of them were walking to the village Emmaus, about seven miles out of Jerusalem. They were deep in conversation, going over all these things that had happened. In the middle of their talk and questions, Jesus came up and walked along with them. But they were not able to recognize who he was.

OBSERVATION

In this story, these are two of the twelve disciples who had walked daily with Christ for three years, and yet, just after the resurrection, they were not able to recognize Him. In fact, even though some of them had just seen the empty tomb, they were not even able to simply believe that Christ had risen. And if you read the rest of the chapter, you will find that while they were talking to Jesus (unbeknownst to them), it sounds like they don't even believe He was the Son of God.

Clearly, this has to be the low-point of faith for these disciples. If there is one thing we can learn from this story it is this: faith...leaks. These were the men who had sailed with Jesus when He walked on water, interrupted a funeral when He raised the dead, and stood boldly before religious leaders when Jesus destroyed their arguments. Surely in those moments, the faith of the disciples was inflated to the maximum.

But now, like a leaky tire, it seems as though all of the air is gone. You see, no matter what history one has with God's presence and even His miraculous touch, we are not assured an overcoming faith based on our past.

IN THE MIDDLE OF THEIR TALK AND QUESTIONS, JESUS CAME UP AND WALKED ALONG WITH THEM. BUT THEY WERE NOT ABLE TO RECOGNIZE WHO HE WAS.

APPLICATION

I must be aware of the weakness of my humanity. My faith level is prone to leak down. It is up to me to continue to build myself up on faith, test my faith and keep believing for more and more from God.

Because faith is like a muscle, it will atrophy over long periods without use. And if I want to strengthen my muscle again, I will have to stretch it by picking up heavy weights and straining myself to do more than is comfortable. Faith is just like that. And you can rest assured Jesus knows this.

That is why Jesus provided His disciples with just such a faith exercise. They were given the opportunity to believe the impossible. As a result, they all become giants of the faith.

You may be asking God why He has allowed things to be so difficult for you right now. But understand this – He is fully in control! He knows just how much your faith can bear, and He will not test you beyond your ability. However, He will stretch your faith muscle to the edge of its ability because He knows that's how faith grows.

TOUGH QUESTIONS THE TEXT DEMANDS

1. Is my faith level currently at an all-time high? Why or why not?

2. What can I do to stretch my faith today?

3. What impossible thing am I currently believing God for?

PRAYER

Lord, I believe. Help my unbelief. Reveal yourself to me in powerful, undeniable ways. Help me to stay in Your presence so I can be close to all that You are doing. And I pray also for a greater gift of discernment. Help me to be able to sense when Your hand is on something and when it is not. Give me the courage to s-t-r-e-t-c-h myself and my faith to the very end. Lord, keep me close to You. Protect my way. Keep my feet from stumbling.

DAY TWELVE

YOU ARE THE
EQUIPMENT

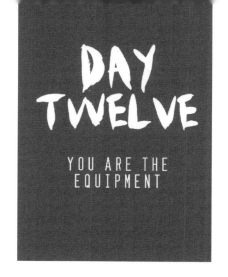

DAY TWELVE

YOU ARE THE EQUIPMENT

SCRIPTURE

Mark 6:7 – 10 MSG
7-8 Jesus called the Twelve to him, and sent them out in pairs. He gave them authority and power to deal with the evil opposition. He sent them off with these instructions:
8-9 "Don't think you need a lot of extra equipment for this. You are the equipment. No special appeals for funds. Keep it simple.
10 "And no luxury inns. Get a modest place and be content there until you leave."

OBSERVATION

Jesus' words are like a field general sending troops into a hostile battle. These men were going into a world that hated the message of Christ, and these men would eventually be murdered for that very message.

However, Jesus' words to them lacked the soft-spoken, apologetic nature that our words may have had.

His instructions were quite to the point: "Take the truth to the people. You, alone, are the equipment. And don't spend the Kingdom's money on yourself."

APPLICATION

Certainly, there are many stark differences in the church system that Jesus began and the church system we inherited in our day. My mind immediately goes to the church of today and how far we have come from Christ's words. Today we have superstar preachers, gold-record producing singers and best-selling authors along with ever-increasing, bloated ministry budgets in local churches and mega-ministries. I wonder if we took these simple words of Christ to the next finance board meeting of most churches, just how many lines we would cut from the budgets?

But there may be an even bigger lesson to learn from this "Jesus story," and it is this: Jesus never intended His message of love to be hindered by a lack of funds. We should be able to find creative, loving ways to spread the message of Christ to the world without leaning so heavily on budgets. And as a believer, I should never let a lack of funding or equipment keep me from doing my part to fulfill the Great Commission. It really doesn't matter if I'm the pastor of a megachurch or I lead a small group at work around my lunch break. Jesus' words are clear, "I am the equipment." His highest commodity in the world today is me and others like me. So we must take that same pioneering attitude that Jesus pronounced over His disciples and go wherever, whenever and however we can to share the gospel to whomever will receive.

1. Can I honestly say that I am Christ's ambassador to those I see daily? Why not?

2. Who do I know in my personal sphere of influence who is yet to surrender to Christ? When will I boldly share the gospel with them?

PRAYER

Lord, help me to grow closer to your heart. I know that Your heart is for evangelism because You love every person You created. Fill me with your Holy Spirit so that I can be as bold as a lion and confident in what You have already placed inside of me. Remind me, daily, that I already have all I need to be your messenger.

DAY THIRTEEN

HEAVEN'S
MEASURING SCALE

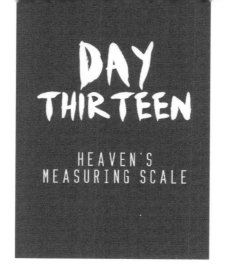

SCRIPTURE

Mark 12:41 – 44 NIV
41 Jesus sat down opposite the place where the offerings were put and watched the crowd putting their money into the temple treasury. Many rich people threw in large amounts. 42 But a poor widow came and put in two very small copper coins, worth only a few cents. 43 Calling his disciples to him, Jesus said, "Truly I tell you, this poor widow has put more into the treasury than all the others. 44 They all gave out of their wealth; but she, out of her poverty, put in everything—all she had to live on."

OBSERVATION

In a culture dominated by pomp and circumstance, hierarchical systems and religion, a simple widow living in abject poverty was nothing more than a nuisance to the geopolitical leadership of the day. Her small offering was less something they would applaud and more something they would have despised.

But Jesus always sees things differently. Jesus told His disciples that this simple woman, who actually gave less than a penny, was the most generous giver of all. Never before had anyone taken this perspective on giving. Not only did Jesus commend her generosity, He actually claimed that this woman's two coins equaled more than the sum total over everyone else's giving combined. Clearly, heaven measures by a different scale.

APPLICATION

I must never lose sight of this bedrock teaching of Jesus Christ. Jesus always found a way to bypass the accepted values of culture and establish His own heavenly value system. He absolutely counts on a completely different scale. He is never thinking about the size of the gift, but the size of the sacrifice. Over and over in scripture, we see where Jesus encourages generosity, but here we are actually afforded the rare opportunity to see what He counts as extreme generosity. And it is not based on the size of the gift. Rather, Jesus sees the size of our hearts. The fact that heaven sees these - and so many other things - so differently, makes heaven a wonderful place indeed.

PRAYER

Lord, forgive me for using man's system of counting. Help me to draw closer to You and learn to see things just as You see them. And I pray for you to release the "widow's mite" spirit of generosity within me.

DAY FOURTEEN

JUST HIS
STUDENT

DAY FOURTEEN

JUST HIS STUDENT

SCRIPTURE

Matthew 23: 1 – 8 MSG

1-3 Now Jesus turned to address his disciples, along with the crowd that had gathered with them. "The religion scholars and Pharisees are competent teachers in God's Law. You won't go wrong in following their teachings on Moses. But be careful about following them. They talk a good line, but they don't live it. They don't take it into their hearts and live it out in their behavior. It's all spit-and-polish veneer.

4-7 "Instead of giving you God's Law as food and drink by which you can banquet on God, they package it in bundles of rules, loading you down like pack animals. They seem to take pleasure in watching you stagger under these loads, and wouldn't think of lifting a finger to help. Their lives are perpetual fashion shows, embroidered prayer shawls one day and flowery prayers the next. They love to sit at the head table at church dinners, basking in the most prominent positions, preening in the radiance of

public flattery, receiving honorary degrees, and getting called 'Doctor' and 'Reverend.'
8-10 "Don't let people do that to *you*, put you on a pedestal like that. You all have a single Teacher, and you are all classmates."

OBSERVATION

In this passage of Scripture, Jesus points out that some of the religious leaders of His day were actually good teachers, and, we can follow their teachings about the Bible. However, he says that you cannot afford to follow them, personally. These are leaders who are too arrogant and think too highly of themselves. They have boiled down all of the wisdom and truth of Scripture to be a bundle of rules designed to load us down. They want to keep the average believers burdened down with rules, regulations and guilt because they believe that in so doing, they elevate themselves. And that is, in fact, what they want more than anything else. They want to be called "Doctor" or "Reverend" and to occupy the places of honor in public gatherings. They want to stand out above everyone else. But Jesus would later say that the way to "stand out" is to "step down" and humble yourself as a servant.

Here, Jesus takes the pressure off of all believers when He tells us that we are not to emulate the behavior nor to covet the positions of these egotistical leaders. Rather, we are to simply desire to be His students. For being His student is the highest place we can attain in His Kingdom.

APPLICATION

To some degree we are all called to be leaders in the Christian community. Whether we occupy prominent positions in the Church today or are simply called to lead by example in school, work and family surroundings, we should all be leading others to Christ. As exciting as this reality is, it can also be a bit of a burden. Each of us has gifts from heaven planted within us, and when we come to recognize those gifts, we are then charged to invest them into God's harvest and produce results...results for God... and that's real pressure.

I know the gifts and talents He invested in me are not there by accident, but on purpose. God truly expects something from me. After all, His word says, "To whom much is given, much is required" (Luke 12:48). And since I have been given much, He requires much more out of me. As noble as this line of thinking is, it sometimes puts undue pressure on us.

Since I'm a Christian leader, I cannot have a crisis or even a bad day. The thought of me being less than positive, even in the face of serious challenges, is just unthinkable. But then I hear the words of Christ, and I am reminded that He is the only Teacher, and I am simply a student. I do have doubts. I am sometimes afraid of how things are going to turn out. Some days I don't feel much like a Christian, much less a leader, and I don't want to even get out of the bed. How can I really be God's called representative to reach His lost sheep? But then I remember that I'm just a student, and He's the Teacher...and then it just looks completely different.

"TO WHOM MUCH IS GIVEN, MUCH IS REQUIRED."
LUKE 12:48

TOUGH QUESTIONS
THE TEXT DEMANDS

1. Do I ever find myself feeling unworthy to be a Christian leader? Looking at what Christ said above, why would I ever feel that way?

2. In what concrete ways can I solidify my place as Christ's student, today?

PRAYER

Jesus, thank You for calling me into Your family. Thank you for elevating me into Christian leadership. I further pray that You find me even more faithful, so I can be used for Your purposes more and more. Forgive me for taking myself too seriously. Help me get through those times that I think I have to be more than You have asked me to be. Help me to always remember that You simply said You are the Teacher, and I am the student. I can always be that, no matter what is going on in my life.

DAY FIFTEEN

WALKING IN
THE SPIRIT

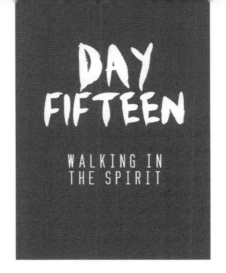

SCRIPTURE

Luke 4:1, 14, 18 NIV
Jesus, full of the Holy Spirit, left the Jordan and was led by the Spirit into the wilderness...14 Jesus returned to Galilee in the power of the Spirit...
18 (Jesus said) "The Spirit of the Lord is on me..."

OBSERVATION

This is one of the most important discourses in all of the New Testament. Luke 4 records that moment when Jesus was catapulted into His ministry and destiny. He spent forty days in the wilderness in prayer and fasting, drawing closer to the Father and clarifying His calling. As He emerged from that sabbatical period, He was more assured than ever of His purpose. He was not only an ambassador sent from Heaven to the lost sheep of Israel. He was, in fact, the one Isaiah prophesied would come to be the Messiah and Savior of the world. It was within this epic moment in the synagogue that Christ revealed His purpose to all in attendance as He read from the ancient scroll and pronounced Himself to be the promised one.

To know one's calling and to boldly proclaim it before others is no small thing for anyone. But here, for the very first time, Jesus makes the kind of claims that will eventually lead to His own crucifixion. This kind of courage and boldness is not human. It comes from a higher source. The Man, Christ Jesus, did not come in the power of humanity; although, He was fully human. He came and operated in the power of the Holy Spirit. The gospel writer, Luke, makes that so clear to us throughout this chapter. He tells us that Jesus did not choose of His own volition to go into the wilderness to be alone with God. Luke says Jesus was "full of the Holy Spirit" and "led by the Spirit" into the wilderness. After the forty days of prayer and fasting was over, verse fourteen says that "Jesus returned to Galilee in the power of the Spirit." And Christ's own proclamation begins, "The Spirit of the Lord is on me..." You see, this entire process was full of and led by the Holy Spirit.

APPLICATION

Since Jesus is the example I am to live by, the clear lesson here is that I absolutely must walk in the power of the Holy Spirit daily. I must not allow myself to operate in man's strength, knowledge, abilities and power. Old Testament prophet Zechariah reminds us that God's will is not accomplished by man's might or man's power, but by God's Spirit. If I am to find my purpose in life and fulfill my destiny in Christ, it will be found only by surrendering fully to the power of the Holy Spirit.

These are abstract thoughts that sometimes lack specificity. So the question begs: "How does one fully surrender to God's will and walk in the Spirit?" For the answer, we need only to look to the life and example of Jesus Christ. As recorded here in Luke four, Jesus took time away BEFORE beginning a new venture to be alone with God. How often do we jump into an idea or project we are excited about only to seek God later when things get difficult? Jesus set the example for us. Seek Him first and often. In fact, throughout the recorded earthly life of Christ, we find Him rising early to spend time in prayer. He is often withdrawing from everyone to be alone with God.

Of course, Jesus didn't have a smart phone to remind Him of all the responsibilities of His schedule. Maybe not, but He did have the greatest calling of anyone to ever live. He was to establish God's Kingdom on earth so that every living soul could hear the gospel of salvation. By the way, He was only given three years to do it and a rag-tag group of twelve disciples to handle the task after His ascension. It worked out pretty well for Him, didn't it? After all, the gospel made it to us two centuries later.

The lesson is clear. We have a purpose that can only be found and accomplished in and through the power of the Holy Spirit. So seeking God's presence must be a daily priority in our lives. I am so glad we have chosen to do that very thing together, today.

1. Since Jesus was lead by the Holy Spirit, I must also be. Honestly, who or what is leading my life now?

2. What concrete things can I do to make room for the Holy Spirit to take the lead in my life?

3. When is the last time I truly withdrew from people, tasks and schedules to give as much time to God as is needed to truly hear from Him? Don't feel guilty about it. Open up your calendar right now and carve out room for Him! You can do it!!!

PRAYER

Lord, thank You for this beautiful time I have with you today. Even though I know I am not perfect, I choose not to dwell on my mistakes while here in Your presence. I am going to dwell on the beauty of this moment. And I ask You to fill my life with Your Holy Spirit. Guide my steps and lead me into the path You have chosen for me. Amen.

DAY SIXTEEN

HOW GRATEFUL ARE YOU?

DAY SIXTEEN

HOW GRATEFUL ARE YOU?

SCRIPTURE

Luke 7:36 – 48 MSG

36-39 One of the Pharisees asked him over for a meal. He went to the Pharisee's house and sat down at the dinner table. Just then a woman of the village, the town harlot, having learned that Jesus was a guest in the home of the Pharisee, came with a bottle of very expensive perfume and stood at his feet, weeping, raining tears on his feet. Letting down her hair, she dried his feet, kissed them, and anointed them with the perfume. When the Pharisee who had invited him saw this, he said to himself, "If this man was the prophet I thought he was, he would have known what kind of woman this is who is falling all over him."

40 Jesus said to him, "Simon, I have something to tell you."
"Oh? Tell me."

41-42 "Two men were in debt to a banker. One owed five hundred silver pieces, the other fifty. Neither of them could pay up, and so the banker canceled both debts. Which of the two would be more grateful?"

43-47 Simon answered, "I suppose the one who was forgiven the most."

"That's right," said Jesus. Then turning to the woman, but
speaking to Simon, he said, "Do you see this woman? I
came to your home; you provided no water for my feet,
but she rained tears on my feet and dried them with her
hair. You gave me no greeting, but from the time I arrived
she hasn't quit kissing my feet. You provided nothing for
freshening up, but she has soothed my feet with perfume.
Impressive, isn't it? She was forgiven many, many sins, and
so she is very, very grateful. If the forgiveness is minimal,
the gratitude is minimal."

48 Then he spoke to her: "I forgive your sins."

OBSERVATION

This has to be one of the greatest of all of the "Jesus stories" recorded in the gospels. In fact, when Matthew tells
this story, he says that Jesus actually commanded that ev-
erywhere the gospel is told this story is to be remembered.
So, apparently, this was one of Jesus' favorite "Jesus stories" as well. There is so much going on in this story: the
lack of hospitality of Simon the host, the strange act of
a known prostitute washing Jesus' feet and drying them
with her hair, and then a simple country rabbi (as they
believed Jesus to be) actually forgiving sins. And as usual,
Jesus is focusing on something completely different than
the rest of us are.

The Pharisees who were hosting Jesus in their home could
not perceive the possibility that Jesus actually knew this
woman was the town whore, yet still let her touch him and
pour her love onto Him. He was teaching us that the vol-
ume of sin means absolutely nothing to Him. Jesus Christ
is so much bigger than the sin, that all sin (no matter what
level) is inconsequential in His presence. All that the Phari-

sees could think about was how big this woman's sin was. But the focus should have been on how big God is. In the end, everyone else in the room saw the enormity of the woman's sin, but she saw the enormity of God's grace.

APPLICATION

Today, Jesus is still far bigger than any sin. I should always focus on what He is capable of doing rather than what I or anyone else has done. Certainly, mankind is capable of colossal sins, but the greater reality is how vast the grace of God is.

TOUGH QUESTIONS THE TEXT DEMANDS

1. Am I guilty of rating sins on a different scale based on how I view them?

2. Are there ever times when I look down on others because of their sins while thinking my sins are less egregious?

PRAYER

Lord, help me see the real You! I want to see the You of Scripture, not the You as portrayed in pop culture or even in religious circles. Help me to see the You that is powerful, bold and gracious. And thank You for being just so!

DAY SEVENTEEN

THE
TROUBLE-MAKING
PREACHER

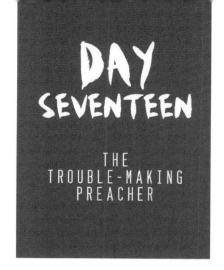

DAY SEVENTEEN

THE TROUBLE-MAKING PREACHER

SCRIPTURE

Luke 4:25 – 30 NLT

25 "Certainly there were many needy widows in Israel in Elijah's time, when the heavens were closed for three and a half years, and a severe famine devastated the land. 26 Yet Elijah was not sent to any of them. He was sent instead to a foreigner—a widow of Zarephath in the land of Sidon. 27 And there were many lepers in Israel in the time of the prophet Elisha, but the only one healed was Naaman, a Syrian."

28 When they heard this, the people in the synagogue were furious. 29 Jumping up, they mobbed him and forced him to the edge of the hill on which the town was built. They intended to push him over the cliff, 30 but he passed right through the crowd and went on his way.

OBSERVATION

In this teaching, Jesus was trying to explain to the Pharisees that He was here for the broken-hearted, not just the religious. But they could not see past themselves. Everything Jesus did was for the purpose of redeeming mankind back to the Father. Here He reminds them that even the Old Testament prophets, Elijah and Elisha, went right past the religious class (Israelites) to reach out to the Leper of Syria and the widow of Sidon. These classes of people were so hated by the Jews that at just the mention of God loving them, Jesus was run out of town and nearly thrown off of a cliff. Jesus was a real trouble-maker to the religious leaders of His day!

APPLICATION

The purpose of the New Testament and all of the "Jesus stories" is not to entertain us, to establish a religion, or even to comfort us. Rather, these stories are here to inspire us to follow the example of Christ in our daily lives. If we go after the heart of Christ, we can expect:

- To be focused on the low class, rejected, unreligious of the community.
- To be ridiculed by the religious establishment.
- To be misunderstood by those who do not have the mind of Christ.
- To be empowered by the Holy Sprit, for we have captured the heart of God.

PRAYER

Lord, give me Your heart. As You once did for the nation of Israel, I ask you to replace our hearts of stone with hearts of flesh so that we can see Your harvest in these last days before Your glorious return. Protect me from the ruling spirit of religion that is still alive and well today.

DAY EIGHTEEN

JESUS SEES THE
REAL YOU

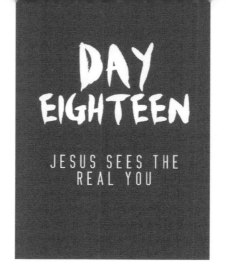

DAY EIGHTEEN

JESUS SEES THE REAL YOU

SCRIPTURE

Matthew 9:9-13 NIV

9 As Jesus went on from there, he saw a man named Matthew sitting at the tax collector's booth. "Follow me," he told him, and Matthew got up and followed him. 10 While Jesus was having dinner at Matthew's house, many tax collectors and "sinners" came and ate with him and his disciples. 11 When the Pharisees saw this, they asked his disciples, "Why does your teacher eat with tax collectors and 'sinners'?" 12 On hearing this, Jesus said, "It is not the healthy who need a doctor, but the sick. 13 But go and learn what this means: 'I desire mercy, not sacrifice.' For I have not come to call the righteous, but sinners."

OBSERVATION

In chapter nine of Matthew's account of the life of Christ, he is given the amazing opportunity to tell the world of his own salvation experience. And Matthew was about as unlikely a character to end up in a "Jesus story" as you could imagine. You see, Matthew was a thief, a traitor and a liar. He was hated by everyone in the Jewish community. He collected taxes from his fellow Jews on behalf of Rome. His paycheck was whatever he could extort from the citizenry above what they actually owed. So it would be just like Jesus to come along and tell everyone within earshot that it is people like Matthew that He came for.

In fact, just saying Matthew's name began the redemptive process in this man's life. You see, for most people, Matthew was a nameless person without a heart. They did not know his name, and they did not want to know it. He was simply known as the "tax collector," and that was as bad as it gets. But when Matthew tells us of his first account with Jesus, he says, "(Jesus) saw a man named Matthew sitting at a tax collector's booth." It may seem like a simple distinction, but it meant everything to Matthew. Jesus did not see a nefarious tax collector. He saw a man who just happened to be sitting at a tax collector's booth. This means Jesus knew that Matthew did not have to always sit in that same seat. Jesus did not define the man by what the man had been doing or what he was even doing at that moment. Jesus knew Matthew was more than what he had become, and Jesus would go on to help him become that saint he was meant to be.

APPLICATION

Jesus does not define me by what I have done or where I am sitting today. The Bible says that before I was formed in my mother's womb, He knew me. And Ephesians tells me that even before God made the world, He loved me and chose me. So whenever I find myself sitting in the wrong place in life, I can be assured of the fact that God does not define me by that snap-shot moment in time. He knows my destiny. He knows my purpose. He created me for greatness, and the disappointments I am facing today will not define the scope of my life.

TOUGH QUESTIONS
THE TEXT DEMANDS

1. Have I forgotten that I am not defined by my worst moment? Do I sometimes let my circumstances tell me who I am?

2. Knowing that Jesus sees my potential and not my failures, how should I redefine my own self-image?

PRAYER

Thank You! Thank You! Thank You, Lord, for loving me enough to see past my mistakes. Thank You for thinking of me before I was even born and mapping out Your plan of peace, hope and potential for my life. I now fully surrender to that plan and I repent of all the times I have accepted a lesser plan because of my fear, rebellion, or guilt. Today, I reaffirm that Your will is to be done in my life.

DAY NINETEEN

JERRY LAWSON, THE SAME YESTERDAY, TODAY & FOREVER?

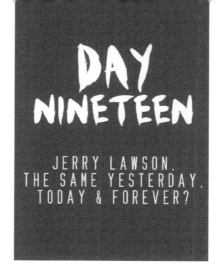

DAY NINETEEN

JERRY LAWSON.
THE SAME YESTERDAY.
TODAY & FOREVER?

SCRIPTURE

Hebrews 13:7 – 8 MSG
Appreciate your pastoral leaders who gave you the Word of God. Take a good look at the way they live, and let their faithfulness instruct you, as well as their truthfulness. There should be a consistency that runs through us all. For Jesus doesn't change—yesterday, today, tomorrow, he's always totally himself.

OBSERVATION

Right off of the top, we recognize that this is one of those oft-quoted Bible verses that preachers and teachers love to emphasize when we are talking about the faithfulness of God, as well we should. However, many times we take a snippet out of the Bible to prove a point we are trying to make, and we forget the greater context of that statement. This is often the case when this verse is used. There are at least three big issues we could notice from this passage. Obviously, the first and clearest lesson is that Jesus never changes. He is the same yesterday, today and forever. But secondly, there is the fact that we should trust and appreciate the pastoral leadership that God has called into order over us in the Lord. However, the most real point that the author is trying to make is the one that we so often overlook - because Jesus is consistently the same, we should also endeavor to be so.

FOR JESUS DOESN'T CHANGE —
YESTERDAY, TODAY, TOMORROW,
HE'S ALWAYS TOTALLY HIMSELF.

APPLICATION

My take-away from this text should not just be that Jesus never changes, but rather, it should be that my goal is to be just as unchanging as He is. I should walk closely with Christ, find my calling and live out that calling as consistently as humanly possible. So not only should I praise the fact that Jesus Christ is the same yesterday, today and forever, but I should also be able to say it like this: "(my name), the same yesterday, today and forever!"

TOUGH QUESTIONS
THE TEXT DEMANDS

1. Am I ever guilty of "proof-reading" the Biblical text and missing the main point? How can I fix this problem in me?

2. Do I sometimes applaud the faithfulness of Jesus while forgetting that He requires the same of me?

3. What are some specific areas in my Christian walk where I am inconsistent?

PRAYER

Lord, help me to be consistent. And in an even greater way, help me to be a model of consistency that others can follow, just as You are for me. Help me to love Your Word and be true to it at all times. I pray that Your Word will speak to me out of its own voice and not just out of my preconceptions.

DAY TWENTY

GOD KNOWS
HIS CHILDREN

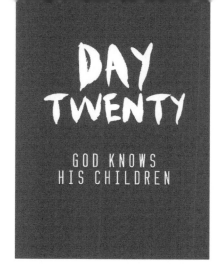

DAY TWENTY

GOD KNOWS
HIS CHILDREN

SCRIPTURE

Luke 16:19 – 31 NLT

Jesus said, "There was a certain rich man who was splendidly clothed in purple and fine linen and who lived each day in luxury. 20 At his gate lay a poor man named Lazarus who was covered with sores. 21 As Lazarus lay there longing for scraps from the rich man's table, the dogs would come and lick his open sores.

22 "Finally, the poor man died and was carried by the angels to be with Abraham. The rich man also died and was buried, 23 and his soul went to the place of the dead. There, in torment, he saw Abraham in the far distance with Lazarus at his side.

24 "The rich man shouted, 'Father Abraham, have some pity! Send Lazarus over here to dip the tip of his finger in water and cool my tongue. I am in anguish in these flames.'

25 "But Abraham said to him, 'Son, remember that during your lifetime you had everything you wanted, and Laza-

rus had nothing. So now he is here being comforted, and you are in anguish. 26 And besides, there is a great chasm separating us. No one can cross over to you from here, and no one can cross over to us from there.'

27 "Then the rich man said, 'Please, Father Abraham, at least send him to my father's home. 28 For I have five brothers, and I want him to warn them so they don't end up in this place of torment.'

29 "But Abraham said, 'Moses and the prophets have warned them. Your brothers can read what they wrote.'

30 "The rich man replied, 'No, Father Abraham! But if someone is sent to them from the dead, then they will repent of their sins and turn to God.'

31 "But Abraham said, 'If they won't listen to Moses and the prophets, they won't be persuaded even if someone rises from the dead.'"

OBSERVATION

In this story, the rich man wants God to send Lazarus back to life to tell his family that God is real, that heaven and hell are real, and that they need to change their ways. But God tells him that this would be useless because if they will not believe Moses and the prophets, they will not even be persuaded when a dead man comes back to life.

Honestly, this does not make much sense to us because it seems that almost anyone would at least listen to a dead man who comes back to life. But God knows His children. In fact, there are many times throughout scripture where the way God chooses does not make sense to His children. But in the end, we always see that He knows the best way.

APPLICATION

I can trust today that God knows me better than I know myself. Even when it seems like God is ignoring me or my prayers, I know that He is doing what is best for my life. I can always rest in the promise that "in all things God works for the good of those who love Him, who have been called according to His purpose" (Romans 8:28). Knowing this, my task is simple: (1) love God, (2) walk according to His purpose. God will take care of the rest.

TOUGH QUESTIONS THE TEXT DEMANDS

1. In those times when God doesn't respond to my prayers and I think He should, how do I react? Do I ever try to take matters into my own hands?

2. Considering the promise of Romans 8:28, what should my simple strategy be?

PRAYER

Lord, I reaffirm today that You always know the way I should take. And I surrender to Your way and Your plan. Help me to better hear Your plan and more courageously choose to follow you 100%. I humbly ask for Your guidance and trust Your way forward. Lead me, Lord. I will follow.

DAY TWENTY ONE

TRYING TO 'OUT-GOD' GOD

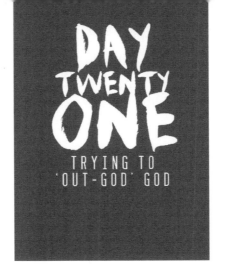

DAY
TWENTY
ONE

TRYING TO
'OUT-GOD' GOD

SCRIPTURE

Acts 15:6 – 11 MSG

6-9 The apostles and leaders called a special meeting to consider the matter. The arguments went on and on, back and forth, getting more and more heated. Then Peter took the floor: "Friends, you well know that from early on God made it quite plain that he wanted the pagans to hear the Message of this good news and embrace it—and not in any secondhand or roundabout way, but firsthand, straight from my mouth. And God, who can't be fooled by any pretense on our part but always knows a person's thoughts, gave them the Holy Spirit exactly as he gave him to us. He treated the outsiders exactly as he treated us, beginning at the very center of who they were and working from that center outward, cleaning up their lives as they trusted and believed him.

10-11 "So why are you now trying to out-god God, loading these new believers down with rules that crushed our ancestors and crushed us, too? Don't we believe that we are saved because the Master Jesus amazingly and out of sheer generosity moved to save us just as he did those from beyond our nation? So what are we arguing about?"

OBSERVATION

The Early Church was experiencing one of its first crises and major decisions. Some of the more conservative believers wanted to require the new "pagan" converts to be circumcised to fulfill the Old Testament Law of Moses. Peter rose up to ask, "Why are you trying to out-god God?" He held that only God could lay these kinds of burdens on His children. In the end they agreed on a few simple requirements that the new believers should uphold just so that the relations could be "congenial" between the Jewish believers and the Gentile believers. Here, as always, we find the good news of Jesus breaking down the barriers that divide and bringing people together around the cross.

APPLICATION

Somehow many in today's Church have completely missed the lesson of Acts fifteen. They are so convinced by what God has said to each of them that they are certain everyone else must share their convictions. We would do much better if we would strive for unity, rather than uniformity. Our task is to just keep our relationship with other believers congenial and agreeable, so we can all focus on the more important issues like reaching the lost with the love and power of Jesus Christ.

1. Do I ever try to play the role of God, demanding what Christian service should look like from others?

2. Have I allowed others to dictate to me (apart from Scripture) what is right and what is wrong in my life?

PRAYER

God, help me to never major on minor issues. But help me to see what truly matters to You. Show me what is near to Your heart so that I can stay close to You always. And thank You for looking past my many weak points to love and accept me as I am.

AFTERWORD

I hope that you have enjoyed this twenty-one day journey with Jesus. My prayer has been that this book would ignite a passion within you to spend more time with our Savior. There is absolutely nothing that you can do that will enhance your life and future more than spending daily time with God and His word. I would like to encourage you to continue your journey with Jesus after you put this book down. And let me further challenge you to bring pen and paper into God's presence each time you enter your prayer closet. That act alone makes a faith statement to God that you are expecting Him to speak to you today.

I have found the "SOAP" method of journaling to be the best for me, so I want to share it with you. I first learned this method from Wayne Cordiero's book *Leading on Empty*, and was further enlightened by *The Divine Mentor*. Below is a simple explanation of "SOAP" journaling:

S — SCRIPTURE
Open your bible and begin to read from the selected portion you have planned for today. Just read and listen for God to speak to you. When you have read today's text, look back for a verse or section that particularly spoke to you and write it down.

O — OBSERVATION
What is God saying to you in that verse? What does it mean? Paraphrase it in your own words.

A – APPLICATION

How does this scripture apply to your life now? Is this a promise, or a challenge, or some instruction for you? Write out how this text applies to you today.

P – PRAYER

This could be a few lines or a detailed prayer request. But remember, prayer is a conversation, so listen to what God is saying back to you. You may want to record it here, so you will never forget it.

You can find more information and resources at www.lifejournal.cc. I have never even met Pastor Cordiero, but his books and resources have done so much for me that I wanted to share this information with you.

However you continue your walk with Christ, just be sure that you place priority on your time with God. Find a quiet location. Eliminate distractions. Set aside a time that you can always give to God. And finally, be prepared to sacrifice something. There will always be something that creeps into that quiet time. You will have to say "no" to some really important things, so you can say "yes" to the best thing.

ABOUT THE AUTHOR

Jerry Lawson met his wife, Leslie, in a small church in their hometown of Eufaula, Alabama. Next came college, ministry and marriage, almost simultaneously. Along the way, God has blessed them with two beautiful girls and a son. But they found their destiny when they launched Daystar Church, along with about 100 wonderful people from Cullman, Alabama. Since that small beginning the church has grown into a large, multi-site church, serving communities across North Alabama. Throughout the years, one thing has remained constant: "Daystar Church exists to transform the community through the love and power of Jesus Christ!"

This church and its people have never been about numbers, but always about seeing the love and power of Christ literally transform individuals, families and communities. Nothing gives Pastor Jerry more joy than seeing what Jesus can do for people who have lost all hope. He often says, "Every religion has its own 'holy book' and shares similar stories, but nobody else has a JESUS!" There truly is no one in the world like Jesus.

Pastor Lawson has also mentored hundreds of pastors through a twenty-four month on-site training process called 24toDouble.org. Jerry is the President and CEO of 24toDouble.org and continues to serve other churches through this non-profit ministry.

The only thing Jerry likes to do more than church and church related activities is spend time with his family on beautiful Smith Lake in Cullman, Alabama. Leslie, Olivia, Abigail and Bryant bring more joy to his life than he ever thought possible.

Made in the USA
San Bernardino, CA
04 August 2014